PRACTICAL LESSONS FROM MY

PROJECT MANAGEMENT EXPERIENCE

Supercharge your PROJECT MANAGEMENT SKILLS

BIREN PAREKH

Supercharge your Project Management Skills

1st Edition

Publication Date: 22nd Oct, 2022

Price: Rs. 349/-

ISBN: 978-93-94808-08-9

Every effort has been made to avoid errors or omissions in this publication. In spite of this, errors may creep in. Any mistake, error or discrepancy noted may be brought to our notice which shall be taken care of in the next edition. It is notified that neither the publisher nor the author or seller will be held responsible for any damage or loss of action to any one, of any kind, in any manner, therefrom. It is suggested that, in order to to avoid any doubt, the reader should cross-check all the facts, law and contents of the publication with the original Government publication or notifications.

For binding mistake, misprints or for missing pages, etc., the publisher's liability is limited to replacement within one month of purchase of the similar edition. All expenses in this connection are to be borne by the purchaser.

The information provided within this book is for general purposes only. The thoughts expressed in this book are the author's own. Therefore, any resemblance is purely coincidental. If inadvertently, we have missed announcing the due credit, future publications will give the due credit to those that are brought to the author's attention.

All disputes are subject to Delhi jurisdiction only.

Dedication

I dedicate this book to my Wife – **Darshana**, who motivated me to writing and for her unconditional support.

Acknowledgements

This is my first book so any comments and criticism are welcome.

Writing a book is harder than I thought.

I will take this opportunity to thank all people who encouraged me.

Firstly, I am grateful to my parents for supporting me in whatever I do. I miss my mother.

My amazing life partner and lady luck, Darshana who has been constant source of inspiration.

My dearest daughter Soumya, who is my biggest critique and supporter.

My little son Yuvraj, whose love enriches my life.

I am eternally grateful to Bharatbhai for patiently proof reading the book multiple times. I also thank Abhay sir for giving valuable suggestions to make this book a better version.

A special thanks to Niraja for giving me timely guidance on few book writing aspects.

I am also thankful to my colleagues, friends, managers, team members for making my professional and personal journey memorable.

Table of Contents

Abbreviations.

AMC	Annual maintenance contract
BA	Business Analyst
BAU	Business as Usual
BRD	Business requirement Document
CCB	Change Control board
CI/CD	Continuous Integration / Continuous Deployment
DBA	Database administrator
EAC	Estimate at Completion
ETC	Estimate to Complete
IT	Integrated Testing
LOB	Line of Business
MQ	Messaging Queue (App Server)
MSA	Master Service Agreement
NFR	Non-functional requirement
OAT	Operations User Acceptance Testing
PM	Project managers, Project Leaders, Program managers, Portfolio managers
UAT	User Acceptance testing

PMBOK	Project Management Book of Knowledge
PMI	Project Management Institute, a non-profit organization to promote project management practice and professionals
PO	Purchase Order
POC	Proof of Concept
PT	Penetration Testing
PWT	Product- walkthrough
RACI	Responsible, Accountable, Consulting, Inform – chart
RAG	Red, Amber, Green Status of the project
RCA	Root Cause Analysis
RFP	Request for Proposal
SDK	Software Development Kit
SIT	System Integrated Testing
SLA	Service Level Agreement
SME	Subject Matter Expert
SOW	Statement of Work
T&M	Time and Materials basis

About the Author

Biren Parekh is an Information Technology executive with over twenty-five years of experience managing and implementing complex BFSI digital transformation programs for top-tier global retail and corporate banks.

Currently a Director at CRISIL Limited (as of June 2022), he is a certified corporate director with multiple global certifications like PMP, ACP, DASSM, PRINCE2, ITIL V3, PSM1, and CSM. He has also volunteered on the IEEE Innovation and entrepreneurship committee and the board of the PMI Mumbai chapter since April 2021.

Being one of the NEXT100 CIO 2020 winners, he is also a regular speaker at conferences and business schools like IIM, SJMSOM, NMIMS, PDPU, and NITIE, where he conducts talks on project management, the Agile framework, Digital transformation and Fintech. He is also an angel investor in several Indian and international startups and even mentors for some of them.

He has been rated in **"Top 25 thinkers on Project Management for April 2022"** and **"Top 50 thinkers in Fintech for Oct 2021"** on the Thinkers360.com website.

Mr. Parekh has published a whitepaper titled 'A Comparative Study of Vendor Selection Process in Global Outsourcing Industry with an Elucidated Scientific Approach' in a reputed Scopus journal. He was also featured in the book 'High Productivity Practices by Successful Leaders' by Dr. Ravindran KA, whereby he shares tips on increasing productivity.

On the personal front, he is a fitness freak and a marathoner. He closely follows equity and enjoys reading, traveling, and exploring new cuisines. In his free time, he publishes articles on interesting topics on his website (bireparekh.com) and LinkedIn. His work has been featured in various magazines, blogs, and PMI journals.

This is the first book he has written to share his experiences on his project management journey.

Disclaimer

- All stories and lessons shared are based on author's personal project management experience. It is not a replacement for any formal project management training. This may or may not work with others, and all lessons should be applied based on the situation's context.
- The humor in the presentation is not to derogate any particular roles, skill sets, country, race, profession, religion, or community.
- All illustrations are created for book except for couple of images which are freely available on the internet and not created by author. No IP rights were violated for the same.
- The presentation does not mean to prove that any of the project methodologies described are inferior or superior to others.
- No confidential information specific to any company, customer, or person has been disclosed. Any resemblance to any person, project, or company is purely coincidental.

Intended Audience

- Professionals reading the book are assumed to have a basic understanding of project and project management-related methodology like Waterfall, Agile, and Scrum, along with relevant terms used in the industry.
- Students taking project management courses may also find it helpful to understand its practical aspects before entering the workforce.
- Author being part of a banking IT Software products company, most of the mentioned experiences are relevant to the software industry. However, it may or may not bear a resemblance to non-IT projects.

Assumptions

- Wherever I have referred as Project Manager, it implies either technical project manager, program manager or portfolio manager and vice versa
- While I have referred to Project Manager in gender neutral manner but wherever I have referred as He or She, I meant it may be male/female or third gender
- I have shared all my learnings in the following chapters. It is quite possible that some of the lessons and practices are already followed in some project or company. So, only some lessons may be applicable to some industry, project, country or company.

Introduction

It all started when one of my LinkedIn contacts approached me a few years back. He had read some of my LinkedIn posts and was impressed with my project management knowledge. About to become a project manager for the first time, he wished to get some project management tips.

We soon got on a call, where I shared my experiences while discussing some strategies to avoid disasters during project execution. Luckily, the discussion helped him sort out his project management issues. After our call, I posted a blog on my website (birenparekh.com) as well as LinkedIn.

To my surprise, the article got a tremendous response.

After twenty-five years of involvement in the IT industry, I've developed some keen insights working with the Waterfall methodology and Agile Projects. Most of this experience stems from my involvement in the product and project implementation of banking products across the globe.

I soon became a part of the PMI Mumbai chapter, where I got an opportunity to share my project management learnings in one of their PM forum webinars. I was elated by the impact I could make in the community. Bolstered by the feedback I received, inspiration struck - which was when I wrote this book. I want to share my knowledge with a broader range of professionals, not only those who attend my sessions or read my posts.

I hope the book will serve as a guide for new, experienced, or aspiring project managers. Typically, most PMs undergo project management training before taking up project manager roles. They are well versed with the theoretical concepts, like the diverse phases of the project lifecycle, knowledge or process areas, and stages of the projects. However, the practical problems of project execution are not taught anywhere or documented in one place. And that is what we are going to talk about in this book.

The waterfall methodology of project management involves the following phases in one form or other:

1. Presales and Contracting Phase
2. Requirements Gathering Phase, also known as the product walk-through Phase
3. Design Phase
4. Development Phase
5. Integration and System Testing Phase
6. Customer testing Phase
7. Production go-live Phase
8. Post go-live support or AMC
9. Enhancements (optional)

These phases often vary from project to project and customer to customer, depending on various factors like:

- The implementation of the product
- The duration of the project execution
- The priorities of the customer
- The commercials involved in the implementation

Even if the project is implemented in an Agile form, some of these phases may overlap, run in parallel, or altogether may not be there. So, several of them may or may not apply to every customer, project, or country.

About the Project Management Institute and PMP

Project Management Institute (PMI) is the leading professional association for project management and the authority for a growing global community of project management professionals and individuals. These professionals and "changemakers" collectively create better outcomes for businesses, communities, and society worldwide.

PMI empowers people to make their ideas a reality. Through global advocacy, networking, collaboration, research, and education, PMI prepares organizations and individuals at every stage of their career journey to work smarter to drive success in a world of change.

The Project Management Body of Knowledge (PMBOK) is not a library, but a guide to the project management body of knowledge. It is generally considered good practice for project management and has been written, reviewed, and edited by hundreds of professionals. The PMBOK guide addresses the entire spectrum of highly predictive and highly exploratory project approaches. The body of knowledge is continuously evolving, with the 7th edition being released recently. Earlier editions were released in 1996, 2000, 2004, 2008, 2012, and 2017.

PMBOK's 7th Edition comprises 12 project delivery principles

1. Stewardship
2. Team
3. Stakeholders
4. Value
5. System thinking
6. Leadership
7. Tailoring
8. Quality
9. Complexity

10. Risk
11. Adaptability and resilience
12. Change

The eight performance domains focus on outcomes and not outputs, supported by models, methods, artifacts, and tailoring the approach.

Stakeholders *focus on Interactions* and relationships

1. The team *focuses on* High performance
2. The life cycle *focuses on* An appropriate development approach
3. Planning *focuses on* Organized, elaborated, and coordinated work
4. Project work *focuses on* Enabling the team to deliver
5. Delivery *focuses on* Strategy execution, advancing business objectives, delivery of intended outcomes
6. Uncertainty *focuses on* Acceptable performances
7. Measurement *focuses on* Activities and functions associated with risks and uncertainty

Preface

Bringing rigor and discipline to the process of Software Development is a long-cherished goal of stakeholders. Various attempts have been initiated for several decades for the same. In the 80's, the concept of SSAD / Software Engineering first emerged. Then came the concept of Software Tools for aiding team members. I was fortunate to have been in this domain and was part of the team that popularized the "Turbo Analyst" CASE Tool developed by Telco (a Tata Company now called Tata Motors.)

Software is said to be an intangible product, and hence, developers think it is a piece of art. Customer requirements are never clearly articulated, and hence in most cases, the "implemented product" doesn't satisfy 100% of the original requirements. It is an essential part of the project management team to deliver a quality product, keeping the cost within the client's budget constraints and deliver the project as per the scheduled timelines.

I compliment Biren Parekh, a veteran in the field, for having come up with an excellent book on this complex subject and articulating his personal experiences. I am sure this book will be read by all IT students, working professionals, and academia.

I wish all the best to Biren and I am sure he will write more books in the years to come.

-Dr Deepak Shikarpur

IT Entrepreneur, Author of 46 Books and Career Counsellor

CHAPTER 0

The Project Manager Unwise or Lazy?

What do you see here? Is the Project Manager too busy or too lazy?

NOTES

CHAPTER 1

Incorrect Estimation

"The only way to reduce the variability in the estimate is to reduce the variability in the project."

- Steve McConnell, Software Estimation: Demystifying the Black Art

In the early stages of the software development life cycle, a project manager or product owner uses effort estimation, a crucial tool to draft project plans and budgets. This practice assists him in precisely envisioning costs and allocating appropriate resources.

According to Forbes, estimation is "an investment that you should factor into software development efforts of any substance."

As it is directly proportional to profitability, effort estimation is the key to the success or failure of the project. When done right, it sails through without any noise. If it goes the wrong way... you might have a disaster on your hands.

Usually, effort estimation is done at multiple levels, known as L0, L1, L2, or L1, L2, and L3 estimation. L0 is considered a very high-level effort estimation, typically performed when the RFP is filled up since it does not have sufficient details for an accurate estimation. In this case, the seller can ask the client for clarifications to chart a precise estimation.

The problem, however, arises when the seller calculates a 'guesstimation' instead, resulting in gross under or over-effort estimation. This is hazardous, especially in smaller organizations that rely on relatively junior team members for their estimation proposals. The practice is not limited to the less experienced, though - sometimes, even PMs fill up estimates based on their gut feeling, mood, or pressure!

Those inaccurate estimates soon make their way into the commercial proposal submitted to the customer, who might rule out the vendor at initial screening if the effort estimation is higher than usual.

On the contrary, if the efforts are vastly underestimated, the client may accept the proposal, thinking it provides a good value for money. In such a case, may God save the vendor, the PM, and even the customer. Such a project can trigger a vicious cycle of project execution with constraints and cascading effects.

"OUR BILL WAS LOWER THAN OUR ESTIMATE."

Once a client awards the project, the vendor opts for a detailed requirement gathering. It is a part of the product walk-through exercise. Only after this step does the PM see the actual efforts required to pull off the project - which could be much more than what they 'guesstimated.' At this point, it is too late to get extra efforts from the management and the consumer: there's already a commercial contract in place, signed on the agreed-upon margin.

There's not much the PM can do at this point: either he sails through the project with fewer resources or seeks management approval to deliver the project within less than the projected frame. As the project gathers pace, this not only burns out the employees but directly impacts the quality and delivery.

PMI data says that 29% of waterfall projects fail and a fourth of the failed projects are due to incorrect estimation.

Lesson 1.1

In such a scenario, the best solution for the PM (or management) is to ask or create only a "Seed SOW." This seed SOW will cover enough efforts to do a detailed product walk-through. It can be the contract to do requirement gathering or effort estimation. Such SOW gives sufficient cushion to PM from the project slipping into the RED.

Let's talk about a different situation. Suppose the vendor estimates the efforts for the requirement gathering workshop but completely omits the preparation efforts while submitting the proposal.

He assumes that preparatory activities like infrastructure setup, setting up customer's business scenarios, and verification of the same, will be done in a single day. This is quite an optimistic view in a product company. This is because in Product Company, major releases are done once or twice a year (comprising a variety of technical stacks and third-party software) due to high complexity of software product or stack.

If the customer shares the case upfront for the demo purpose and functionality is not available in the system, the same needs to be executed by tweaking the existing software product or preparing wire-frames to give a '*true demo*' feeling.

This may take time, and it is grossly underestimated when effort estimation is done. This ultimately results in burning midnight oil before the requirement gathering workshop, and it will also result in being unable to set up some of the events for demo purposes. In either case, the team somehow makes it but with red-eye on the first day of the requirement gathering workshop.

Lesson 1.2

It is imperative to estimate realistic efforts to prepare for the requirement gatherings workshop and include them in the overall project plan. This may be possible only with experience. Alternatively, pro-actively prepare the environment when at peace.

Another thing that PMs forget during requirement gathering is taking into account their team's competency. Most PMs make far-fetched assumptions that newbies will catch up in no time as a part of pair programming. However, building resource competency for a complex algorithm or product isn't possible overnight - it takes anywhere between a few weeks to a few months unless you want them to break the code instead of *building* it.

Lesson 1.3

During efforts estimation and project planning, the PM should budget and highlight the realistic time required to build team proficiency. Add it as a risk without fail if majority team is new and highlight it in your status report during the project execution. Keep a tab on it. Risk management is covered in a separate chapter later.

Although PMs often budget in various factors during project planning, sometimes they forget about the technology stack in the proposal. His team could be working with its previous versions or may not even be familiar with newer stacks. Some software is also licensed, making it impossible to use it off the shelf. Although it depends on the agility of the company and the multi-level approvals required, sometimes it takes up to four weeks to procure such software - resulting in slippages right at the *start* of the project!

Hurdles like this can often be mitigated by opting for cloud infrastructure, but that comes with its challenges. This is why factoring in time for procurement makes a considerable difference - without it, one is as good as planning the project for failure.

Lesson 1.4

Understand the project infrastructure requirements, i.e., hardware and software from peers or PMs running similar projects. Consider the realistic lead time required to procure infrastructure and avoid any slippages in the project plan.

I once observed a situation where the software required was incompatible with the open-source libraries it was being used with. This happened after the proposal was approved and the customer requested a POC. During the offshore testing, the developers realized that their licensed software simply *did not work* with the open-source SDKs they used. Now, it could have been possible that the version of the library the customer requested was new. However, something like that can set off a disastrous chain of events.

First, the developers scramble madly to make it work, which delays the process depending on how long it takes. Then, people start looking for scapegoats (or even a new project or job!) The PM ultimately ends up revising the technology stack while trying to avoid being penalized or offsetting the costs.

Lesson 1.5

Never commit to a hardware-software list (installable/products) without validating their version compatibility from engineering team with proof.

Chapter Summary - Estimation

Incorrect estimation is at the heart of several project failures. This results in budget over run or significant delays in the project execution. Hence, it is imperative that estimation is done as precise as possible.

The best way to perform estimation is to take past lessons from similar project executions in your organization, industry or LOB. For new projects, it's advisable to do some kind of POC before doing the complete estimation and presenting it to the sponsor or board for budget approval. The ETC and EAC need to be reviewed on important milestones or at periodic intervals. This allows timely course correction and brings back the project on track.

NOTES

CHAPTER 2

Lack of Clarity in Requirements

"A lack of clarity could put the brakes on any journey to success."

- Steve Maraboli, Life, the Truth, and Being Free

Successfully delivering the solution is one of the most important milestones in any project journey. Most projects start with requirement gathering and end with a developed solution that closes the gap.

Some companies undergoing digital transformation take the help of consultants or System Integrators to articulate their requirements. However, others don't. The issue arises when even the stakeholders providing the requirements are not clear. As a result, when the RFP is floated, sometimes, the requirements are just one or two sentences long. They are sometimes longer but not articulated well enough to understand. Some requirements just point to gaps in existing legacy systems - but they fail to realize that those gaps won't exist if a new system is implemented!

Maybe they lack the time, but often, they go into solution mode without holistically understanding the business, product, or LOB.

Instead of stating the *problem statement*, they just state the *expectations*.

This results in an RFP void of sufficient details for the proper solution and estimation.

While preparing the RFP response, more competent vendors consult the customer for more information to understand requirements. This helps them understand business expectations, undocumented things, or the rationale behind those requirements. However, in the worst case, they frame their response by making assumptions based on the requirements, leading to incorrect effort estimation as well.

Sometimes, people who estimate efforts aren't even a part of the project. They might move out of the department, LOB, or even the organization. This leaves a void once the project is approved and the execution starts. Due to the lack of handover and absence of such people, the new PM will be literally at God's mercy. They manage to confront business users and safeguard the vendor's interests if they are seasoned. If not, they'll be putting out fires until the project ends.

Knowingly or unknowingly, few customers often take advantage of such situations. If the new PM is not assertive, scope creep soon takes root. It starts with stakeholders wanting to add just *one* element. When the PM does not maintain airtight control on such changes, the Business Analyst (BA) or Product Owner (PO) might add it to the requirements document... followed by increasing demands to add it to different places like inquiry screens reports and extracts. One small change eventually starts getting reflected in multiple places and, not to mention, adds to the efforts. This is, of course, an optimistic scenario with only one added component.

Now, imagine this situation with multiple changed components.

The result is *devastating.*

What starts out as an extra touch point here, an additional screen there, and several other such changes lead to cascading effects in project efforts which can derail the project budget, schedule, and even the margin. Due to the negligence of his predecessor in considering the extra efforts, the new PM now needs additional efforts and time to complete the project.

Lesson 2.1

In such a situation, the PM should take an affirmative stand in such a situation. He should highlight the RFP gaps to the customer stakeholders and management. He should introduce them as Change Requests. Otherwise, he may lose credibility with the team and encourage scope creep.

Now, think of a situation where the PM, who estimates the efforts is the one who has to execute the project. He will not have any excuse to blame anyone/predecessor because of poor estimation. How can he escape from the same?

The best solution for any PM during such high-level estimation for RFP is to get as much understanding as possible from the customer. He could schedule a call or keep adding assumptions in the RFP response document. This ensures a way out to consider any deviation from the assumptions as change requests. If possible, the PM can also add an example of his understanding of the requirements. Including a complete list of requirements in the contract demonstrates how the effort estimation has been carried out. Chapter 9 talks about contracts in more detail.

Lesson 2.2

To avoid ambiguity, it is best to include the complete list of requirements and assumptions in the contract. This can help prevent scope creep and gold plating.

The purpose of requirement gathering is to clear the air around ambiguities in the requirements. Nevertheless, the right stakeholders are often not present during those meetings. Ideally, one would not like to proceed unless things progress as per the published plan. However, one cannot always progress sequentially in today's agile world. Businesses need to start realizing business value from their new projects as soon as possible. In some extreme cases, PMs or management stall the exercise of requirement gathering altogether, leading to delay, conflict, and chaos. Hence, it's best to avoid stalling the project unless explicitly agreed upon in the contract.

Those requirement gathering meetings must happen, even when the requirements are unclear during the requirement gathering or PWT phase. It's a good idea to document any assumptions and mention that *any* change to them would result in a change request. Make sure it is recorded in the minutes to ensure all spoken words are documented.

These minutes are circulated daily to all the stakeholders, including attendees and absentees. Explicitly stating assumptions, make them crystal clear, and pave the way to make any deviations as change request down the line.

Lesson 2.3

Despite scheduled discussions, if requirement gathering remains incomplete, the best way is to document it with assumptions and publish it daily to avoid conflicts later.

Situations like the above almost always result in the customer coming back with changes. Unless a contract with open scope has been signed, these changes are considered as change requests. The requests also need to be highlighted in the periodic status report. It's best not to commit to these new CRs unless you want to derail the project schedule. Instead, they should be kept in the back pocket and traded when required. Alternatively, these can be committed to later if you get additional resource bandwidth, or they can be used as a tool for customer delight. In fact, you'll be surprised by the length of the list by the end of the project!

Sometimes, customers escalate the criticality of newly discovered CRs and insist on them going live. In such cases, be smart and play the trump card by asking to reduce the criticality of existing CRs or negotiate the code drop, go-live date, or budget.

Lesson 2.4

The best way to beat the situation where requirements are unclear due to a lack of stakeholder participation is by adding a lot of assumptions and examples to the Requirement gathering document.

Chapter Summary - Requirements

A good number of projects fail because of requirements that are incorrectly captured or missing key points. Good clarity in capturing requirements is an essential element for project success.

It is always better to identify a business analyst or SME upfront before starting the project and ensure continuity until the end of the project. However, considering various factors, it may not be always possible. In such cases, strong documentation about requirement gathering and doubts raised during the requirement gathering is essential to avoid project failure. This includes classifying all the requirement gathering discussion in different categories like discussion points, clarification, updating documentation, Nice-to-have types. Put actionable against each point, make relevant person accountable, validate it, notify the impact on testing and delivery cycles, trace it to closure, and compare it against the RFP response to identify scope change.

NOTES

CHAPTER 3

Lack of Stakeholder Identification

"When trust is high, the dividend you receive is like a performance multiplier, elevating and improving every dimension of your organization and your life.... In a company, high trust materially improves communication, collaboration, execution, innovation, strategy, engagement, partnering, and relationships with all stakeholders."

- Stephen Covey

Stakeholders are those people and entities that are directly impacted in one way or the other while executing the project. Even the people working *on* the project are a part of it - like the operations team, regulatory reporting team, legacy technology team, legal team, migration team, network team, as well as the vendor, sponsor, customers, or government agencies interested in the end outcome.

It is common to see PMs missing out on identifying stakeholders during the early stages of the project. However, engaging stakeholders at the right moment with the right intention and intensity is vital. Otherwise, no matter how hard you work to execute the project, it can still yield poor results. Famous examples include Enron, Maharashtra (India) or the Tata Nano plant, West Bengal (India), and the opposition by the Australians to mining and exporting coals from the Carmichael mine in Queensland State. Thanks to the local citizens' resistance, they had to withdraw their setup with huge losses.

The situation can quickly become messy when stakeholders are identified at later stages. There's a chance that those stakeholders could oppose the project execution, which could set it back by weeks, or even *months*. There's also the danger of the project cost being overrun.

Let's not forget: situations like these put the reputation of both, the vendor and the client at risk.

This forces the PM to go back to square one, understand the new requirements, and derive its implications on the cost and schedule. He even needs to go to the sponsor to seek approval. Not only is this embarrassing for the vendor organization, but it also reduces their chances of cross-selling or up-selling. In some cases, the negative publicity can even get them black-listed for future prospects in the client organization, country, or region!

Hence, it is paramount to identify the stakeholders and engage them constructively.

Many data privacy-related requirements are ignored during the requirement gathering stage, particularly in banking projects. When the vendor is a BFSI expert, the customer often expects the data privacy standards to be de facto and be addressed without saying. This is only discovered later during the testing phase (SIT, UAT, or OAT.) Due to criticality, they have to be fixed overnight because of compliance issues.

Situations like this can often be avoided right from the start when the project is about to get signed. When the PM comes on the board, he should identify *every* deliverable committed to the customer, even the trivial ones. These need to be added explicitly to the contract Annexure. Once that is done, the PM should ask the client organization, who will sign off every deliverable to mark it as complete.

This exercise often hints at who the actual stakeholders are.

Add all those stakeholders with their names and designations in the project kick-off meeting and request them to be present during the requirement gatherings workshop. Most of them are high-level executives who nominate someone from their department to attend instead.

Ensure you document this during the meetings, circulate those minutes, and request the stakeholders' presence during the requirement gathering workshop. This seals your position on identifying stakeholders. At the same time, get a commitment from the sponsor that no other stakeholders are required to be identified. That will double seal your position. Going forward, all stakeholders are updated about upcoming meetings and minutes. Always keep them in the loop. Any new stakeholders identified later can be treated as CRs.

This is only possible if the PM is assertive and has done proper documentation right from the beginning. It works well, provided they're on top of their communication history and can pull out mails or minutes related to any previous discussion.

Lesson 3.1

The best way to identify stakeholders is by listing all deliverables in the contract and asking the sponsor about the people responsible for sign-off at the end of the project kick-off meeting. This will ensure that all stakeholders are identified early in the project during the requirement gathering phase.

Chapter Summary - Stakeholders

The stakeholders are key to project success, as they are the only living being out of all resources that will be used for the project. Any miss outs may cause huge damage or impact the viability of the project.

It is essential to engage stakeholders right from the beginning until the end of the project because they influence your project outcome. The stakeholders may increase or decrease the risks as they perceive different value for themselves compared to others. So, it is not only important to manage and monitor stakeholders, but equally important to engage them through regular communication using a communication management plan. Transparency is required in setting up expectations upfront and ensuring that project outcomes are very well understood by each stakeholder and that they are on the same page.

Effective stakeholder engagement will not only set you on the track to success but also ensures peace of mind for stakeholders, sponsors and the organization.

NOTES

CHAPTER 4

HR & Team Management Issues

"Human resources are like natural resources; they're often buried deep. You have to go looking for them; they're not just lying around on the surface."

- Ken Robinson

In IT companies, resources are the critical assets that must be managed. They should be handled with the utmost care, passion, and empathy. Some firms know it better than others. Those firms grow exponentially, much higher than the industry average.

Usually, when a client approves the project, the PM starts running helter-skelter to get resources from internal or external sources. Due to this pressure, compromises are often made in the quality of the hiring process.

As per Tuckman's model of the four stages of team effectiveness, 'Forming' is the crucial phase of team building. The team members' roles and responsibilities might be unclear since this step focuses more on *people* than the work. Unfortunately, this stage is often overlooked. Many PMs and management rarely show empathy to their team, considering them as 'entities' instead of human beings with feelings, likes, dislikes, and moods.

This is why most PMs underestimate the lead time required to recruit and induct team members into the project. However, this isn't as easy as plug-and-play. The lead time to have a new team member settle down in the company or a project is a must to ensure they become a team player. Therefore, HR often asks new members to join only on particular days when they have a buddy to talk to.

When a new team member is inducted, their first few days (or weeks) are a lot like orientation day at college. During their induction, they must go through the company orientation, product overview, etc. It is the PM's job to handle the new team member's issues, which includes understanding their expectations and emotions and considering the best way for them to contribute to the project. They need to review the project timeline, the current status, burning issues, etc. Otherwise, he risks facing low morale right from day one. Attrition is highest in the first few days if a new joiner is not carefully mentored or attended to!

The next step should be to formally introduce the new teammate to the team and give them time and space to set up their workspace. Subsequently, he should be given a session on the project documentation and an overview of some of the work done in their area before he can start working on it. And Yes, this should be done in first month itself else new joiners feel that they are not being attended to particularly when they have jumped the ship.

Unfortunately, the real story is quite different. A good number of PMs expect the new team member to churn out deliverables from the very next day. Sadly, many management seniors think one can deliver or be efficient only under pressure. They do not understand that having such unrealistic expectations results in burnout as soon as the team member joins the project. Sometimes, seniors even seek deviation to skip induction of new joiners! However, this kind of deviation should not be given, particularly when a person has newly joined the company.

If the PM has overwhelming expectations from a new team member, the problem starts from day one itself. Ideally, they need to clearly and cleverly budget the required time for a new joiner to catch up. Depending on the company's size and agility to bring new members up to speed, this time often varies - but anything less than two weeks is usually a disaster waiting to happen.

Lesson 4.1

The PM needs to budget time in the project plan to induct team members into the project. This may include time to settle down, understand the work culture, and undergo orientation and domain training. The PM should raise these issues when there is pressure to bypass the team-building period. Failure to budget the team 'Forming' effort is a ticking bomb.

In one of the multi-million-dollar projects I worked on, the original plan developed in March was to go live in the last week of November. The go-live date was agreed upon six months prior. Unfortunately, I overlooked the public holidays mentioned in the project plan. Thanks to resource issues, the project was already running late, and UAT/SIT had to be squeezed in a short time. Needless to say, we were also facing quality issues, and a lot more had to be fixed in a short time to meet the deadline. However, the worst was yet to come.

All the hell broke loose six weeks before the target date.

This was when I discovered that a few key members had planned their leaves due to the festive season of Diwali. Having not asked them about this beforehand, and due to their reluctance to cancel their plans, we failed to fix the critical issues on time. Banks undergo a change freeze during December, as we all know. This made us push the go-live to January end.

This was one of the biggest professional blunders of my life - a whopping two months' delay since I had overlooked the team's public holidays and leave plans. I hadn't attempted to check the dependencies of the main team members or create backup plans. From then onwards, I asked the team to fill up a monthly leave tracker for planned leaves during the next three months. This helped me to keep an eye on the leave plan and approve or disapprove leaves upfront by keeping the project go-live in mind.

This is why PMs need to keep an eye on the leave plans of their team members and check the team schedule at the start of every quarter or two quarters in advance. Overlooking a small, thoughtful step like this can often jeopardize the project.

Lesson 4.2

The PM needs to keep a watch on upcoming festivities and public holidays and leave plans for at least one or two quarters in advance to keep the project schedule on track.

Most PMs prefer to keep their work-life limited to the workplace. While it is good to separate personal and professional lives, some do not even acknowledge their team members outside the office. It's not that only you, as a PM, should know your team members - even teammates should know each other and be able to get along. This is the 'Norming' stage of Tuckerman's model. It is natural to have some disagreements occasionally, but not to the extent where it leads to animosity towards peers.

In one of the overseas projects I worked on, I was taken aback when two of my team members started fighting at office over something which had happened outside the workplace. I had to separate them with the help of other team members. Had it not been for the timely intervention, someone would have surely been hurt! Not to mention, issues like these often raise doubts regarding the lack of collaboration among the team and the manager's interpersonal skills.

Therefore, occasional team-building and bonding activities are a must so that team members can know each other better. Do not overlook this at any cost, even if you have a fire-fighting situation. If you're short of time due to work pressure, convey plans to the team - give them something to look forward to. Keeping aside a small monthly or quarterly budget for these activities is good. You can request HR for this, or even you, as a PM, can spend it as a professional expense to successfully deliver the project.

Lesson 4.3

The PM should schedule and budget team building and bonding activities to maintain harmony and the fun element in the project.

In another instance, I was asked to travel at short notice to a new country for a project. I couldn't figure out why I was asked to travel as a PM was already executing the project on-site. The only thing I could sense was that either my domain expertise was required or that the customer had raised some serious concerns. Although it was a frigid region, I agreed to travel to that country since I was told that the project was small and wouldn't take more than a couple of months to go live.

Only when I landed did individual team members approach me, privately appraising me of the situation and the mess created by the present PM. He had made a lot of unrealistic commitments to the customer under pressure without consulting the team members about its feasibility.

When the delivery date was around the corner, we were falling flat due to over-commitment and unrealistic expectations, along with a massive pile-up of issues. There was much ambiguity around the deliverables. Whatever was delivered was also not as per required quality. The team was just trying to do coverup instead of working in harmony. This was our first implementation in that country, but the repeated slippages and poor quality had left the customer dissatisfied and frustrated. We were about to be thrown out of not only the bank but also from the country.

I figured out the reasons behind this mess in less than a week. The previous PM lacked interpersonal skills and wasn't a team player. While not knowing the domain was also his weakness, I typically discount it - you can usually find a workable solution without deep understanding if you ask the right questions.

First, I prioritized the issues in the backlog by working closely with each team member and hearing their views. Some tough decisions had to be made. Some of the customer's unreasonable demands forced me to say *no*. Fortunately, we successfully executed and delivered the project in the end! It also reached the second phase, which was a much bigger pie. We entered that country with a rousing success. This was in 2009 when Agile was not popular; hence, backlog was never a common terminology.

Lesson 4.4

Interpersonal skills are inevitable for project success. Aspiring PMs or existing PMs should develop these skills to execute the project holistically and successfully.

Chapter Summary - Team management

Henry Ford said - "Coming together is a beginning, staying together is progress, and working together is success."

As they say, the strength of the team is each individual member. The strength of each member is the team.

One of the most challenging tasks of the project manager is to see that team works collaboratively to accomplish a shared aim in the most efficient and effective way. It is his responsibility to identify the strengths and weakness of the team and distribute tasks accordingly. He is expected to choose and deploy the best strategies and practices for the team rather than the naive adoption of 'populist process'. It is expected that the project manager provides autonomy to the team and empowers them.

However, his job doesn't end there. Straightforward situations are rare when dealing with human resources. Every team is unique and will face unique situations. The project manager is expected to display compassion and empathy during such situations. He should continuously reflect and correct the team engagement strategy. Remember, no 'one-size-fits-all' and you need to adapt the best strategy to help the team collaborate naturally rather than forcing them to do it.

The project execution should become a team sport to successfully navigate to the timely delivery.

NOTES

CHAPTER 5

Governance Oversight

"Get the right people. Then no matter what all else you might do wrong after that, the people will save you. That's what project management is all about."

- Tom DeMarco

In some cases, the existing PM might leave the organization unexpectedly due to work pressure or reasons like health or family. In some cases, the project might have been approved suddenly to exhaust the available corporate budget. There may be incessant pressure from the customer or top management to start the project (obviously to start billing), which is why the PM might have been pulled into the project at short notice.

Guards often have to be changed between projects. If the new PM is soft-spoken or unfamiliar with the domain or organization, he will be cautious while dealing with stakeholders in the initial days. He might not know much about the 'Power and Interest' grid related to stakeholders' engagement. In such situations, the salesperson and outgoing PM bombard him with project documents accumulated since the start of the RFP stage. A planning meeting follows this. In short, he hardly gets any time from the management point of view to understand the project-related nitty-gritty.

This situation reminds me of the following joke.

A rich guy (say, Tom) was having a party at his house. Tom had everything: money, a big house in Beverly Hills, drugs, cars, planes -- anything he wanted. Tom was also eccentric, and he had filled his pool with crocodiles.

Tom and his friends were all drinking, getting high, and partying next to the pool. Tom got up on the lifeguard tower, and all his friends looked up.

Tom called for silence and said, "OK, the first person who swims across my pool will get all my money."

No one moved. Tom looked over the crowd, drew on his joint, and said, “OK, the first person that swims across my pool gets all my money and my house."

Still, no one stirred. "OK then, the first person that swims across my pool not only gets my money and my house, but all my cars and planes too."

When no one responded, he said. "OK then, my money, house, cars, planes, all the dope you can handle, properties, stocks, bonds, and investments, you can handle everything I own."

"Splash!" Someone had leaped in the pool.

At once, the Crocodiles swam towards him, but the man rolled over like Tarzan -- he was all over the place, fighting and dodging. Finally, he got out on the other side of the pool.

Tom on the tower ran to him. "That was incredible! I never thought I would ever see this day. Do you want the money now or later?"

The man replied, "Later - I first want to know who pushed me!"

Similarly, the poor PM has to start somewhere - and must keep juggling various tasks simultaneously. Sometimes, he may even forget to assign tasks to his team members. I recall a classic example of this during one of my product walkthroughs. During the meeting, the PM had not informed the SME to note down minutes or action items. The SME had assumed that the junior BA would do it. The junior BA felt that PM would do it or assign it to someone else. It took a few days before the PM realized that there was a gap in terms of expectations between team members.

This is why publishing and explaining the RACI chart is necessary when you have a new team or are preparing test cases or releases.

Occasionally, such blunders can be corrected. But sometimes, it is too late to cover up. Some of these incidents can often result in rework or even damage reputations.

Ultimately, the PM is responsible for the results, and this behavior may cost him his job!

Another such incident occurred during the first product implementation of one of my projects. Along with the product team, I had defined high-level responsibilities for the team. However, we forgot to highlight the people responsible for preparing the training material and handling the training itself. Since the BA of the project team was part of the implementation for the first time, he didn't pay attention to it from a trainer's perspective. After much negotiation, the SME took over the training, albeit in a delayed manner. Later, we agreed that the BA would look after it subsequently. Since this point had never been articulated in the project kick-off document, there was much hesitation around it from the beginning.

Lesson 5.1

The PM must clearly define the RACI chart for all big or small deliverables while assigning all tasks. This helps in avoiding any confusion. Moreover, the responsible person can focus their attention on it right from the beginning.

When I was a newbie PM, one of my biggest mistakes was not to keep my seniors appraised of the project's progress. As a result, any issue or escalation came as a surprise to them. I didn't want to overwhelm them by feeding them the smallest events but was reprimanded for not keeping them in the loop. This caused a lot of awkwardness for me - I had to justify all my steps and the rationale behind the escalation.

If you receive dozens of emails from your juniors every day (especially when there are several), it might not be possible to read all of them or get hold of all conversations outside mail exchange. Communication is key - find a way to update your managers and key stakeholders clearly, concisely, and articulately.

During a particular overseas implementation, we migrated branches to the core banking platform almost every weekend. With so many branches going live, the account migration often had issues. Once or twice a week, batch processing would abort. This was a severity level *1* issue - if we failed to fix it, the end-of-day processing wouldn't be complete, and those branches wouldn't be able to open the next day. I was always so worried about the batch abort and getting it resolved that I often forgot to keep key stakeholders in the loop. As a result, they would often escalate to my boss in India, and I often heard from my head.

It became my second priority to justify the steps I was implementing to address those issues. However, the process of keeping everyone updated soon became exhausting. After a few such incidents, I learned my lesson: as soon as any batch abort occurred, I would SMS all key bank and company stakeholders. Every fifteen to twenty minutes, I would also send them updates about the problem's current status and the steps being taken to resolve it. This helped me concentrate on the issue at hand while keeping everyone on the same page, which was soon appreciated. As a plus, if the stakeholders had any suggestions or solutions, they would revert right then, making my job easier.

To avoid burnout due to communication, PMs should invite all stakeholders to the project kick-off meeting and publish all the scheduled governance level meetings. Knowing whom to contact in case of Severity 1 issues is also important. Add seniors and team members' names as applicable in the kick-off deck and highlight the frequency, and type of progress reports publishing mechanisms like push, pull, call, or one-to-one meetings. It's easy to seek feedback on the proposed governance structure, communication plan, and publishing of progress reports. Get buy-in from key stakeholders, document it, publish the minutes and religiously follow that. That's all.

This gives a green light to the project manager to keep publishing project status as applicable periodically. Project status updates may include.

- Weekly working-level team meetings (internal and external) along with a status report
- Dashboards to reflect the project status, risks, key issues, milestones, and dependencies.
- Stakeholders who will receive updates during Severity 1 and 2
- Monthly (or bimonthly) status update meetings with the senior stakeholders over a call
- Quarterly meetings with the top management meeting which are often face-to-face and supported by the executive deck
- Green days (Number of days in a month without any incident)

It is *imperative* to publish status reports to different stakeholders at an agreed frequency, irrespective of whether the meeting was physical or virtual. This is the starting point to establish your foothold on the project.

Management often tends to delegate this responsibility to the tech lead, who is often so busy that they often forget to publish those reports or do so with stale updates. When things go wrong, fingers are pointed at them, even if they're the only ones juggling multiple tasks on hand.

Lesson 5.2

Never ever forget to set up the governance structure and reporting mechanism at the start of the project. Ensure that as a PM (or next in line), you regularly and transparently publish the project status reports and schedule periodic meetings.

From a governance perspective, once you have agreed on the project plan, it is important to keep track of it as a part of monitoring and controlling the project. You should immediately highlight any deviation to stakeholders and update the RAG status accordingly. Corrective actions should be sought from the responsible team members.

Because of issues at their end, clients often unilaterally reschedule the go-live timeline without formally seeking consensus or informing the vendor. Sometimes, even the vendor misses out on this due to poor communication. Instances like this are rarely noticed, sometimes only through a chain of forwarded emails.

Ultimately, it is the PM who's blamed for the ineffective communication. If any such incident is noted, such deviations should immediately be highlighted in the next weekly status report, and the project RAG status should be marked as Amber or RED. Sometimes, if the PM feels that only a certain aspect of the project is RED, he can instead show the RAG status of each project management area like the scope, schedule, financials, or efforts. This makes it easier for management to understand the status of the different aspects of the project.

Lesson 5.3

The PM should fearlessly inform the management about any unilateral deviation from the agreed-upon baseline by the customer and highlight the same in a periodic status report. Any possible corrective actions and impact should be listed or kept open until evaluated. Unless the status and its impact are not highlighted correctly, the PM will not get support from stakeholders and managers at a later date.

Consider a situation where the key stakeholder has a magnetic, almost overbearing personality, and the PM is meek. A stakeholder like this can play to his strengths by using his charisma to overshadow the PM's authority. He might even be prone to giving too much theoretical direction and ultimately derailing the project.

I had a stakeholder like this on one of my projects. He used to give a lot of unsolicited advice to PM and the team, carrying out shadow project management and wishing that everything happened on time without considering the practical constraints or bottlenecks in the system. This went on to the extent that more advice for the next step would already be thrown at us before executing the current step. The worst part was that this magnetic stakeholder barely knew anything about the product or implementation lifecycle!

His charm spellbound top management. As he drew a huge pay packet, the organization felt he was giving valuable advice. This became a problematic situation for the PM. Whenever the PM executed anything, it sounded like he had done it due to that key stakeholder's advice and not on his *own* merit.

Of course, this looks innocent from the advice perspective. But it becomes too much for the PM or program manager later.

Many times, some of the senior stakeholders don't even have any relevant project experience. Often from tier-1 or Ivy League MBA schools, they command the key position purely due to their connection with top management and charisma.

A preferable way to handle such people stepping on everyone's feet is to expose them and let them give unrealistic commitments and unwanted advice to the customer. Without any experience or focus on commitments, they're all bark and no bite. Let nature run its course, and the customer will realize the truth, after which they'll start sidelining them too. It's best to remain a silent executioner in situations like these where speaking up directly is riskier.

Lesson 5.4

Let charismatic and exaggerating stakeholders face the customer and fall flat on their loud talks sooner than later.

As a part of the pre-PWT workshop, in one of the projects, we had highlighted the need for the expertise required by stakeholders for a different session. PWT was planned to last for four weeks. Hence, the right stakeholders needed to be present during different sessions to complete it on time.

One session was about interfacing with legacy systems and migrating the customer data into our systems. We planned a three-day session in the second week to capture the required details. We planned to cover pending doubts in the subsequent week before we signed off the requirements in the last week. IT folk couldn't join the workshop in the second week. They had proclaimed emergency leave. We were informed that someone else would pitch in. But, when we asked queries to the stand-in person, she was lost. She was more into production support. As a result, she was unable to give enough information as required. This session snowballed to the following week. We could not complete documentation in time and get sign-off in our last week. This resulted in delays associated delays in completing the milestone. The contract completion sign-off got delayed by two weeks, spilling over to the next quarter. I am sure everyone understands the importance of closing the deal before quarter-end. So, my mistake of not raising the Red (or even Amber) flag at the first instance resulted in delays in deal signing.

Lesson 5.5

Without much ado, highlight the lack of participation/resources from the customer perspective right from the start of the project, irrespective of the phase of the project. This can be primarily done through scheduled periodic governance calls and publishing status reports highlighting red flags and risks associated with delays.

Chapter Summary - Governance oversight

Project governance is not just about micro managing the project. Rather, it is about setting the operating framework, defining clear boundaries about acceptable variance and ensuring that the project execution meets its organizational and strategic outcomes.

It is centralized control that is required to ensure that the project delivers desired outcome and intended value. Project governance is the primary role of the Project Management Office (PMO). It is quintessential to have lean, agile, and light-weight governance that focuses on successful project delivery. Holistic project governance should focus on finance, quality, security, data, user experience, legal and regulatory, people, operations, infrastructure and more apart from defining the authority to approve changes and make other business decisions. It should provide an integrated structure for evaluating change requests, risks, issues and dependencies associated with the project delivery ecosystem.

NOTES

CHAPTER 6

Risk Management

"Risk comes from not knowing what you're doing."

- Warren Buffett

Every day, right from the time you wake up until the time you go to bed, there is a risk involved in everyone's life. Many people don't realize this. Unseasoned PMs often overlook risk in their projects, assured that they can take everything in their stride.

Risk management involves making and carrying out decisions that minimize the adverse impacts of risk on an organization, projects, and people. The PM must identify stakes and possible threats while planning the mitigation to ensure a well-managed project.

Most of the time, the PM might just superficially highlight some risks such as:

- Chance of missing deadlines
- Requirements not being clear
- Resources not being available

Many companies have dedicated departments and committees for risk management. Their sole job is to cover all areas under risk management by identifying risks and impacts, calculating their probability of occurrence, and working on strategies to mitigate them.

Problems start surfacing when the risk becomes much more tangible, and things start going down the hill. During review meetings, the senior management soon starts questioning the PM about risk materialization. They often want to know:

- Whether risk mitigation plans were in place
- What would be the impact on the budget, schedule, and scope
- Why this risk was not perceived, if the risk was not included
- The plans to mitigate the risk

This kind of risk materialization may even result in the PM or team losing the job, the company losing its goodwill, or may also bring down the organization. Hence, it is *crucial* to highlight risks in the status report along with their impact and mitigation plan.

The PM should stress various categories of the risks with sub-risks. This includes various categories like vendor, process, product, program, organization, customer, requirements, operations, compliance, information security, environment, and infrastructure.

The PM needs to:

- Define the order of the risks
- Define primary and secondary risks
- Identify sub-risks within each risk
- Define factors for rating impact and probability and contextualize the project scenario to justify them
- Define weightage for the impact of various risks and assess their probability
- Figure out exposure to various risks and categorize their severity
- Define mitigation plans for reducing the impact and prepare a contingency plan
- Track the risk status till project closure.

This risk assessment must be carried out religiously, once every fortnight or month. This ensures that all risks are captured, reviewed, and highlighted, and that mitigation plans are prepared and tracked to closure. Without this exercise, the PM gets beaten up when things go haywire.

In one of my projects, we had just completed the code drop (post-development), but the customer had not started the testing. When we had a status call with customer PM, he informed us that the test environment was being used for the UAT of another project. Unfortunately, we did not document or highlight this anywhere.

Once the testing started, the customer said that the software quality was terrible and impacted their business plan to go live by the planned date. This, in turn, had resulted in an impact on business revenue. He escalated it, although the defect density was less than 1%.

The lack of availability of the testing environment caused thrice the time delay caused due to quality issues. We had *never* highlighted the environment issues as a risk when they occurred. It could have helped us avert escalation and have given us ammunition in the form of risk impact to shoot down the customer's claims.

Once, we were implementing the product version for the first time for this customer. I didn't highlight that the release might have poor quality and stability issues during the customer testing phase. When the customer reported many issues, this put me in reactive or defensive mode. Instead, I should have proactively appraised the management about expected escalation due to perceived risk upfront. Had I highlighted it in time, this situation could have been avoided.

In another instance, I once failed to highlight the interdependency with resource-constrained product groups. This was normal in most product companies; hence I overlooked it. Since I didn't emphasize the risk in my project status report, my project couldn't receive timely support at a critical time to fix internal defects. This caused a cascading impact on delayed delivery to the customer. Obviously, the buck stops at me and so did in this case.

Lesson 6.1

Ensure every possible risk should be thoroughly assessed, analyzed, and brought out internally and externally in the different governance forums.

Chapter Summary - Risk management

Risk management requires continuous review with a risk register at weekly meetings. The project steering committee should set up an acceptable risk appetite and risk threshold upfront and review it continuously through RBS and Risk-adjusted backlog. Failure to mitigate the same challenges successful delivery of the outcome.

As they say, one of the PM's eyes should be on possible risks and the other on the project execution. The organization can standardize possible risks category-wise and ensure that they are reviewed in periodic steering committee meetings.

NOTES

CHAPTER 7

Inadequate Quality Focus

"Quality in a service or product is not what you put into it. It is what the client or customer gets out of it."

- Peter Drucker

Quality is an essential dimension of our day-to-day life. We never want to compromise when paying for some product or service. When a product fails to meet quality expectations, we contact the seller at once to either replace or rectify it. We lack the patience to wait for a longer duration. Products of poor quality make us question how the vendor can provide such a pathetic quality. While buying, we expect the seller to have tested it and pass it through stringent quality control before putting it on the market.

The same feelings exist for buyers of software, I presume.

However, over the years, we have accepted that no software can be perfect or 100% defect free. There is always scope for improvement.

Take, for example, the many crashes of the Boeing 737 MAX. They were caused due to the quality issues attributed to the software defect. Similarly, software issues at British airways in 2020 caused considerable disruption of flights. These, and many other cases, demonstrate that quality is of utmost importance for any software.

It is prudent to discuss the expected quality with the customer upfront and agree on the expectation. A piece of software perceived to have quality issues by one customer might still be of better quality to another customer.

Recently, I read about an issue in a well-known European bank where payment processing happened twice, charging the customer twice as well. This shows that even software in the most prominent companies is not flawless but rather, is 99.99999% defect-free.

One should discuss the testing strategy with the customer during the product walkthrough. Based on my experience, the answers to the following questions should be addressed and well documented. This will help to have clarity of thoughts on both sides. This gives the customer a clear idea of the expectations and will ensure minimal surprise when the testing starts. The list includes -

- What will be the different kinds of testing, and how will each be carried out?
- Which testing phases will be conducted by the customer, and what will be the sequence of these phases?
- Will there be an overlapping phase?
- How will configuration version control be done during overlapping phases?
- What will be the entry and exit criteria for each testing phase?
- How many defects can remain open at one time?
- What would be the defect severity level (Severity 1, Severity 2, Severity 3, etc.) before moving to the next phase or round of testing?
- What can be the expected defect density (defects per number of test cases, number of lines, or number of function points) in terms of percentage for each round of testing?

- What is the projected number of expected defects?
- What percentage of defects can be expected to be reopened?
- How many testing cycles can be expected for different testing phases?
- If migration is involved, how many rounds of migration testing will be carried out?
- Will migration be tested using the complete set of production data or the sample data?
- What hardware and software will be used during testing?
- Is the hardware used for testing shared and agreed upon?
- What are the dependencies for executing each testing phase?
- What will be the duration of each testing phase?
- Have local holidays been considered in the planning of testing durations?
- Is proof of offshore testing required? If yes, is there any specific template?
- Will any data (mock or production) be available to the vendor offshore for testing?
- Which automation testing software will be used by the client?
- Will any automation scripts be used? If yes, is the vendor expected to provide the scripts?
- Is the automation testing software used by the client the same as that of the vendor?
- Who will be the SPOC for each round of testing or each testing phase?
- Will the vendor have access to the testing environment (servers, database, etc.)?
- How soon can the client share the test cases with us?
- Does the client require help in preparing test cases? Is that effort budgeted in the plan?
- What will be the location and time zone of the testing execution team so the vendor can align support accordingly?
- Who will sign off the test completion report at the end of each phase or each round?

- If migration is involved, will testing be done on migrated data?
- What kind of governance will be used for defect triaging like daily calls or meetings?
- Is the testing dictated by the vendor during the testing strategy discussion in line with what has been agreed upon in the contract?
- When will the testing walkthrough discussions be held?
- Will sample interface files with real (masked) data be provided for offshore testing?
- What will be in scope and out of scope?
- At what point will security and penetration testing be conducted?
- What are the limitations and risks involved?
- What are the training requirements, if any? Will it be conducted before or after UAT is carried out?
- What are the assumptions?
- What kind of defect tracking tool will be used?
- What kind of defects severity is expected?
- How will defect severity be decided?
- What will be a logical test calendar?
- What will be the SLA for addressing defects in each phase?
- Who will be responsible for each activity of testing?
- What documentation and records will be maintained?
- How long will the test documents be retained?

I hope this gives you a broader idea of what type of information should go into the testing strategy. If well documented, it ensures harmony and connection between stakeholders - everyone knows what to expect. An escalation can quickly happen in case of deviation if the PM doesn't give a rationale or take corrective action. This is why PMs should spend significant time with the Test Manager to craft, sign off, and execute the testing strategy.

I have got a buy-in from the customer using the above areas that have helped me to sail through difficult or delayed projects. With clear expectations, the customer does not need to escalate the issues.

Lesson 7.1

It is imperative to develop a clear testing strategy, document it, and get a sign-off before the code drop is done. The absence of this is the sure-shot recipe for failure unless you have a 'super-team.'

Humans often tend to make assumptions. Sometimes, being busy planning the implementation and managing the delivery challenges, PMs can forget the customer's point of view. This happens mainly when the implementation team is relatively new to the product.

Once, I noticed that a customer had prepared incorrect test scenarios for SIT and UAT. It was only when testing started that several issues were reported. In fact, these were not issues - these were gaps in the customer's understanding. This occurred due to the customer's lack of adequate knowledge about the new product.

We reconducted a week-long workshop for the client's testing and business teams to educate them about the product workings and scenarios. Considering the understanding gap, the washout ratio stood at 15% during the twelve weeks testing cycle. The customer team had to prepare test scenarios and test cases from scratch before they could resume testing. This resulted in a 20% schedule overrun!

As soon as the customer is ready with the test scenarios and test cases, a walkthrough should be scheduled with all stakeholders, including the vendor. It should be the PM's responsibility to check with the customer about the status of the test case preparation and push to schedule a walkthrough with them. Once the vendor reviews the test cases, they should share their honest feedback to ensure that all the stakeholders are on the same page.

Lesson 7.2

Plan to conduct a walkthrough of test cases with the customer as soon as the testing strategy is finalized and before actual customer testing starts. This will iron out understanding gaps to a large extent.

In one instance, a customer proposed a change in the requirements to develop a few reports. Since this was a complex change, we needed time. Once we customized and delivered the report, the customer complained about its format. Based on their geolocation, they wanted us to write monetary amounts in million-dollar and format dates differently. These were cosmetic changes; however, there were a few other issues. They also wanted changes in the length of certain fields and how they should break when account details were displayed.

When developing deliverables (including documents), the PM should get it validated with the customer during the development or offshore testing phase. Customer feedback should be obtained *before* the completion of actual code drop or offshore testing.

The PM should plan to showcase deliverables to demonstrate progress, either online or offline. This can be in the form of screenshots, sample reports, or anything verified by business users. This helps to nail the perfect first-time-right delivery. It also reduces the defect count during the initial testing phase and saves any delays.

Getting customer validation and verification on reports or interface files is crucial. In the same way, a functional demo of the software helps a lot to get agile feedback. The PM should budget some time for the same in the project plan.

Lesson 7.3

Always plan the showcase of deliverables much earlier than the code drop milestone date. This helps to carry out course correction (if any) and mitigates the risk of an incorrect understanding of the customer requirement. The efforts to lay out the deliverables should be budgeted in the overall project plan.

Chapter Summary - Quality management

Quality management is one of the twelve principles of project management. It is imperative to build quality into process and deliverables. Quality may have different dimensions like conformity, reliability, uniformity, satisfaction, performance, efficiency, sustainability, resilience and even more. The cost of quality should be always considered when trying to meet the project outcomes and should be budgeted into the project commercials. It is one of the most common and frequent miss outs in project estimation.

NOTES

CHAPTER 8

Ineffective Communication

"The result of bad communication is a disconnection between strategy and execution."

- Chuck Martin

After signing a contract, Sales and management sometimes ask the PM to take over the project at once. This can happen before the PM has a chance to even ask about skilled and sufficient resources. Top management usually wants to ensure that the media and the stock market take notice of the numbers. Everyone has their priorities: forcing the PM to pick up the ball before it drops from their hand.

This is something that happens due to improper and fragmented communication in most teams.

No one bothers to check if the PM has enough breathing time to understand the project in totality. Sometimes, a different PM or interim delivery lead may be involved at the Presales and Sales stage, but he might not even execute the project. The management starts looking for the right PM once the contract is signed. However, this varies on the client tier and can result in inexperienced people being assigned to the project.

When the new PM enters, he does so right in the middle of the project planning or execution phase. At that point, his highest priority is to get an actual idea of *what* has been committed to the customer.

Unfortunately, sales and prospective customers often carry out soft commitments without record. They may communicate outside mail, over drinks, or in meeting rooms to win the deal. The PM goes by the contract given to them, so they aren't even aware of those discussions!

This is why the PM should always request a formal handover note from Sales (or their predecessor) before entering the project. They need to take some time to research before getting into execution mode. Most top management state they do not have time to explain history and geography - insisting that the PM learn on the fly. This is where instead of strategic mode; one starts getting into tactical mode. Irrespective of pressure, the PM should ensure he receives the handover document, or he can prepare one before starting the project. It may have a checklist like the one below:

- Proposal/contract
    - Are current and past RFP documents available?
    - Are proposal documents available?
    - Did the management approve effort estimates?
    - Was any demo organized? If yes, were they Screen-based (mock-ups) or application-based?
    - Are any demo-related documents available?
    - Is there any agreed-upon SLA for different phases of the project?
    - Is there any signed MSA available?
    - Are minutes of the meeting available for all formal customer engagements?
    - Was a technical proposal or solution document given?
    - Are any open points from the contracting stage available?
    - What are the existing, proposed, and agreed-upon hardware configuration and software versions?
- Requirement gathering documents
    - Is any shared BRD available?
    - Is the RFI or RFP document available?
    - Were there any interface specifications shared?
    - Was there any reports specification shared?
    - Was any NFR requirement given by the customer?

- Are all commitments listed in the handover document?
- Were there any open items from the requirement gathering phase?
- Are there any documents pending to be submitted by the customer?

➢ Project Management documents

- Was the project kick-off done with the customer? Are the presentation deck or meeting minutes available for the project kick-off meeting?
- Do we have internal project kick-off documents available along with the deck and minutes?
- Is any revision carried out regarding efforts?
- Are any change requests pending to be addressed?
- Are there any identified risks and their mitigation plans?
- What are the roles and responsibilities of the team members?
- Any open positions to be followed up on with HR?
- Any management commitment open and to be followed up on?
- What is the Project RAG status at the time of handover?
- What is the exact status of the project as published to all stakeholders?
- Where are the past customer status reports?
- Where are the past internal management reports?
- What is the license agreement?

➢ Billing

- What is the agreed-upon billing process?
- How is billing supposed to be done?

- What is the invoice-raising process?
- What are the projections?
- What is the required SQA compliance, and by what date of every month?
- Are there any outstanding invoices?

➢ Version control

- Which current configuration version of the product is committed to the customer?
- Are all project management-related documents maintained in the repository?
- Where are the configuration version branch details?
- Any there any open action items regarding version control?

➢ Testing Strategy

- What are the different types of testing agreed upon with the customer?
- How will the customer report defects?
- Is there any dashboard where defects and their status will be published?
- Were any commitments made to the customer during testing?
- Do we have to provide Proof of Testing to the customer? Where is the template for that, if any?
- What will be the SLA for fixing defects during the testing?
- What is the NFR strategy?
- What is the status of defects as of now?
- Are defects triage calls taking place? What is their frequency?
- Do we have access to the customer's environment?

- Customer details
    - Who are the key stakeholders, and what are their roles and responsibilities?
    - Is there any escalation matrix defined and agreed upon?
    - What is the frequency of publishing customer status reports? Are the same reports shared with internal management and the team?
    - Are different meetings being conducted as per the mentioned Governance structure? Where are the Minutes for each type of project meeting?
    - Are there any special customer commitments done to the customer?
    - Are there any past customer complaints? Any open or pending complaints?
    - Was there any escalation by the customer in the past?
    - What is the customer's skill set level?
    - Are they sufficiently staffed?
    - Are there any risks highlighted by the customer?
    - What is the equation between the different stakeholders (business, technology, operations, etc.) on the customer's side?
    - Is there any political situation from the customer's perspective that one needs to be aware of?
    - Any undercurrents among stakeholders?

- Resources
    - What is the resource plan?
    - What is the recruitment plan?
    - What are each member's roles and responsibilities?
    - Are resources adequately skilled?
    - Do we need to impart any training to resources?

- What is the backup plan for key resources?
- Are any commitments made to the resources regarding promotion, roles, or on-site deputation?
- Are resources trained as per the linguistic language required for customer interaction?
- Is there any leave plan shared by resources?
- Are there any commitments made to resources, for e.g., rotation of project or group, etc.?
- Are there any pending performance appraisals?

➢ Development/Support Handover

- What are the offshore and on-site server details?
- What is the debugging process?
- What is the security mechanism?
- What are the support hours?
- What are the contact details of the support team?
- Who all are support persons from the customer?
- Which is a template for the release note?
- Where are the past release notes?
- Where are the Impact Analysis and RCA documents stored?
- What is the CCB process being followed?
- Who are all the key CCB members?
- What is the existing deployment architecture?
- What kind of CI/CD exists?
- Is there any data migration planned or pending?
- Where are the past mails or mailboxes?
- What are the phase-wise or tranche-wise commitments?
- Are there any known patterns of issues because of migration or pending defects?
- What are the third-party software integration tools agreed upon?

- What are the Information security specifications decided upon?
- Where is the deployment guide?
- Where is the summary of recently completed releases or activities?

Few or all of the points above apply to any handover, depending on the situation: from sales to implementation, from the outgoing to incoming PM, or from the implementation PM to AMC PM. Any new PM taking over the project should get hold of as many details as possible from the above list.

If enough details to execute the project are unavailable, the PM should raise caution in their internal management status report. He should mention the lack of adequate knowledge transfer as the highest risk - this will bring it to the management's attention and give the PM some breathing space.

In one of my projects, the management asked me to travel and take the handover from my predecessor. The project was nearly half executed. In my enthusiasm, I agreed - without waiting to understand the nuances, issues, and gaps. To my horror, the skeletons in the closet tumbled out as soon as I took over. This turned out to be my worst nightmare. Since I hadn't asked them to list down the burning issues, I wasn't aware of daily escalations. The team was not competent enough to address all the issues. I soon realized that escalation was an everyday affair. I often lost my sleep over the lack of a proper handover. From that day onwards, I prioritized receiving a formal and detailed handover before taking over a new project.

Lesson 8.1

Any PM taking over the project should ask for a detailed handover per the checklist above. Failure to get a thorough formal handover may result in heartburn later.

Some PMs often misapprehend project performance as their personal performance. This results in them trying to hide the actual status of the project. 'Watermelon status reporting' describes the phenomenon where the RAG status of the project appears to be green from the outside.

But if you dig deep, it's actually *red.*

False reporting happens for several reasons. Sometimes, the PM might be a novice, or he might just not want to admit that things are not going as they should. Projects with a risk of being canceled also fall prey to this practice. Even higher-ups' resort to pulling strings to ensure it is not reported as red. No matter the reason, watermelon status reporting disguises the project's actual status, hiding the serious issues to ensure project continuation and avoid the stakeholders' scrutiny.

Some stakeholders prefer watermelon status report. This is because they don't want a PM to report a project as red. In such case, they would have to investigate the root cause, which might lead them to have their own flaws exposed. There will be also some stakeholders who will try to correlate the data from different slides of (watermelon) project status report to find the veracity of the content and prove that this is watermelon status report.

I am sure, many of us will defend that it can also be cultural values of an organization to do this kind of false reporting.

All said and done, providing a transparent status report is tough. It takes tremendous courage to challenge the status quo and bring about a more significant mindset change. Although project performance should not be misconstrued as personal performance, it can often make or break the PM's career. Has anyone ever received a 'meeting expectations' or 'meeting above expectations' rating during performance appraisals when their project status is red?

Never!

While behavior like watermelon status reporting is often approved by the management in the early stages of a project, it results in unrecoverable damage later. When the project fails, the same management blames the PM for the fiasco. This is why the PM needs to be cautious and point out all the relevant details in their transparent status reports.

I often faced scrutiny while reporting the transparent project status in my management summary reports. When I mentioned resource shortage, my senior demanded the status of work done by each person daily. He wanted to determine if I was speaking the truth and monitoring the resources. Such micromanagement overwhelmed the team, but I resolved to continue with transparent status reporting, which finally helped me meet my objective and get more resources.

If any senior demands watermelon status reporting, ask them to put the request in the mail. Their hesitation to do so immediately puts a stop to this request. Always stick to the factual data in the management status report. That is what will help you in the long run.

Lesson 8.2

Never indulge in watermelon status reporting. The PM's primary responsibility is to display integrity in reporting the actual status through transparent status reporting.

In one of the projects, I worked on, a crucial team member caught typhoid. This, coupled with the usual attrition, made it impossible for us to achieve the delivery date committed to the customer. While I had discussed the revised date with the team, I had not yet conveyed it to the customer. We were still sending status reports to the customer with the unrealistic delivery date.

Before I could get around to informing the customer about the delay, one of my team members conveyed it to them during a call. Understandably, the customer was furious and escalated it to the highest level.

When I talked to my team member, he said that since we were discussing delays, the customer had a right to know. I knew this was my fault: since I had not shared the customer status report with the team members, they were unclear about what was disclosed to the customer. Plus, I should have informed the customer as soon as we discovered the discrepancy.

This is why I now encourage PMs to share customer communication with their team members: either in the same mail or during the stand-up or internal status call. Sharing a summary with the team about these updates keeps them up to speed, preventing confusion and unwanted escalation in the future.

Lesson 8.3

Transparently and regularly share customer communication and interaction with the team to avoid confusion and disconnect. During the internal discussions, ensure the team knows the clear boundaries about what they should disclose to the client.

When good news arrives, the PM is often the first to know and cannot wait to break it to the management. However, the situation is almost the opposite when bad news is received. The PM tends to avoid sharing it with the stakeholders, fearing that they will shoot the messenger. This hesitation leads the PM to secretly hope that the stakeholders learn of it themselves. In situations like this, they often resort to watermelon status reporting. Once the key stakeholders start looking carefully, they'll soon realize that the project is red deep down.

The PM doesn't realize that his job is to opt for transparent status reporting, no matter what. His responsibility is to seek corrective action, not shy away from it. The project needs to be back on course. They fear being labeled inefficient if they report the project is red, but that's not a genuine concern if they add value by mitigating the risks and taking corrective action.

Bad news should be announced as soon as possible. There's an old saying that if the first thing you do each morning is to eat a live frog, you'll have the satisfaction of knowing you're done with the worst thing you'll have to do all day. Brian Tracy's 'Eat That Frog' emphasizes that eating a frog is a metaphor for tackling your most challenging task for the day. As our day starts, we are at our most energetic, so taking up the most challenging job first is often the best idea. The sooner you crack bad news, the faster you can start taking corrective action.

Lesson 8.4

Do not hesitate to report RED RAG status as and when required. The sooner you break the bad news, the faster you can start course correction with the help of supportive stakeholders.

When I started out as a PM, I didn't follow any clear plan for communicating with my stakeholders. When the project was in green, I would publish the project status report first thing in the morning. However, when things were bad, I tended to go for watermelon status reports or avoid publishing them altogether, hoping the stakeholders wouldn't dive deep. I was so scared of messing up that I avoided them and my boss as much as possible, going so far as to use a different coffee machine!

However, doing this is not an option in the long run. Thankfully, I've started taking things in my stride over the years. As a part of the governance structure, I have developed a clear communication plan for keeping all my stakeholders updated.

- For my project team – a daily stand-up call, twice in the initial days if you are a new PM or on a new project
- For the customer's project team – a daily triage call, if customer testing is in progress
- For the working group along with the customer – a weekly status report, followed by a call
- For the sponsor – a fortnightly status report, followed by a call
- For Governance – a monthly status report, followed by a call
- For Production support – a monthly status report, can be fortnightly post-go-live for some time
- For Senior management – a fortnightly status report with financials
- For SQA – Monthly updates
- For Top management – a monthly summary status report

- For the cross products team – A status mail twice a week on key Issues and dependencies with aging
- For the finance team – monthly accrual numbers

All the frequencies mentioned above can change depending on the status of the project and as per the project communication plan.

These different status reports help to have a communication plan that is clear, defined, and easy to follow. It leaves out ambiguity and ensures that a proper audit trail is maintained and followed. After all, good communication is indeed the bridge between confusion and clarity.

Lesson 8.5

One of the first things the PM should do after taking over the project is to define a communication plan. As a part of that plan, they should assign responsibilities to key team members to publish or communicate the transparent project status regularly to relevant stakeholders.

Chapter Summary - Communication

Broken communication results in visible disconnect and confusion among stakeholders. The Project Manager should ensure structured and frequent communication between the stakeholders including the team about various risks, issues, dependencies and the overall project status. It is the key to stakeholder engagement. Relevant communication models should be adopted as per the audience and culture's needs. It is advisable to have a communication management plan developed at the initiation stage and publish it during the project kick-off meeting seeking feedback.

NOTES

CHAPTER 9

SOW/Contract

"Basically, managing is about influencing action. Managing is about helping organizations and units to get things done, which means action. Sometimes, managers manage actions directly. They fight fires. They manage projects. They negotiate contracts."

- Henry Mintzberg

Contracting is the most important thing in any project. It should be paid the utmost attention to avoid losses down the line. A salesperson usually prepares the contract by copy-pasting, then takes a few key inputs from delivery, after which the legal team is asked to review it. The salesperson's top priority is to close the deal as soon as possible, while legal wants to align the contract terms with the organization's risk appetite. Often (though not always), contracts are prepared as fast as possible without deep thought. The ultimate scapegoat will always be the delivery team if something goes wrong. This is why the delivery head should devote attention and time to go through the contract in as much detail as possible - ensuring a fair and timely delivery.

In the early years of project management, I was not well aware of contracting terms and conditions. This caused a few issues during project execution when a customer showed me the contract. When I actually started going through the contract, I had to read every sentence, trying to work out alternate interpretations and reading between the lines. This led me to construct different scenarios and figure out how they would impact us in the worst case. This painstaking process resulted in me building a checklist that I use to verify contract terms and conditions quickly.

The PM or contracting team sometimes resort to ambiguity, overlooking clear roles and responsibilities. Preparing a RACI chart to list the people responsible for various tasks and sub-tasks is essential. When prepared at a high level, such charts can be interpreted very differently by different people. Hence, making the chart as detailed as possible and listing even the minute phases and subphases is paramount. It is also necessary to note down how stakeholders will provide support for a particular task.

For example, consider the data migration phase. The vendor writes the scripts, but the customer's IT team executes them. Operations verifies the reports, and the customer's users carry out the test (SIT or UAT) execution. It is imperative to explicitly put this down in the chart and detail what kind of support will be provided for incidents and defects.

Based on the vendor's commercial agreement, the contract should include who will oversee L1 and L2 support and their exact responsibilities. The vendor's team supervises L3 support, but one should often list these aspects in the contract depending on the customer's requirement and commercial agreement.

Lesson 9.1

Define and review the roles and responsibilities of L1, L2 and L3 support in the contract. A small mistake can cause a bunch of issues in the maintenance and support mode at the later stage, impacting profitability and NPS.

While executing one of my projects, we had to implement a new product and prepare commercials for it based on the effort estimation. We budgeted a warranty of one month and prepared commercials based on it. After the high-value contract was executed, we started the implementation. Since we committed to a warranty period of one month in the contract, we pulled out resources when the project went live at the end of the month.

This didn't go down well with the customer.

He mentioned that as per the Master Agreement, we had to provide three months of warranty support. We were not allowed to pull out resources. This was a real shocker since it involved a considerable number of resources and we would lose around 7% of projected profitability if the extension were granted.

Since we were bound by the Master Agreement, we didn't really have a choice. Ultimately, we had to give in and extend warranty support.

While working on estimation and calculations for the contract, you should always consider the Master Services Agreement and prepare a new SOW and commercials accordingly. While I learned this lesson the hard way, I hope you don't have to.

Lesson 9.2

Before finalizing any contract, refer to the Master Services Agreement if applicable, to see if any specific terms will impact the new SOW.

Including penalties in the contracts is a standard practice. It's an age-old trick to attract serious vendors and ensure vendor commitment. Although the customer has a right to demand a fine for slipping SLAs, the vendor also has an equal right to present his viewpoint and requirements.

How should one calculate the penalty? One needs to understand the terms and conditions of the penalty and that it varies from situation to situation. The vendor can request the customer to start the clock once he gets the necessary information to analyze an issue. However, the buyer should stop the clock while the vendor waits for the details. This should also be documented in the contract.

The vendor can also request the following information before the clock starts ticking:

- Logs (application, server, OS, database)
- Screenshots
- Data that caused the incident
- Server version details (OS, database, etc.)
- Configuration of hardware and software
- Third-party software details like browser used
- User details
- Actual output (reports or interface files)
- Steps to simulate

Lesson 9.3

Before signing any contract involving a penalty, one needs to understand thoroughly the conditions that involve a penalty. Ensure that the required details are available before penalty conditions can be agreed upon.

One of my customers requested a project plan in their contract. They were well within their rights to request it, but there was a catch.

Our project plan showcased hard-coded dates for events like the code drop and go live. However, a legal issue delayed the contract signing by three weeks. When the project kicked off, and the project planning discussion started, the PM from the customer's side insisted we stick to the code drop mentioned in the SOW!

I vehemently disagreed. Such situations are inevitable when Gantt charts are prepared in Excel. As the contract signing had been delayed, the other dates too would have to be shifted. After much more escalation and negotiation, the client finally agreed to move the go-live date.

This taught me that one should never ever agree to enter the hard-coded date in the project plan. Instead, use terms like Month 1, Month 2, Month 3, or Week 1, Week 2, Week 3, etc. Once both parties sign the contract, Month 1 or Week 1 starts from that date onwards. While using this method, make sure you include an additional clause in the contract that this is a tentative plan and that the final plan will be configured after the project kick-off meeting.

This strategy keeps the vendor protected while portraying a realistic picture. I have seen situations where contract signing takes as long as 3 to 6 months and even a year, particularly for banking deals. If the deal size is large (> $5-10 million), it may take even longer.

It's possible for equations to change in the time between preparing the contract and signing it. This is why buffer time is essential - it saves the customer and the vendor from getting into an imbroglio later about hard-coded dates. In case of a delay from the customer side due to their internal issues, the vendor PM will be able to charge the customer on a T&M basis if there is a separate clause to penalize. So, this kind of project plan and clause in the contract will create a fortuitous situation for vendor.

Lesson 9.4

If the contract requires a project plan, you should include relative dates, not absolute dates.

As discussed in Chapter 1, often a customer requests to include requirements list in the contract. Most of the time, the requirements (CR) list would be one-line at the time of signing the contract. If a vendor is smart, he would have done detailed analysis before signing the contract. He will have a realistic efforts estimate. Otherwise, a vendor would have done only high-level efforts estimation. The cost of these Change request (CRs) are included in the contract most of the time. However, since the requirement provided at the RFP stage is at a very high-level (one-liner) it is quite risky to include even its high-level costing in the contract. As mentioned earlier in chapter 1, one should do the high-level estimation with some basic assumptions. These assumptions should be also included in the contract if the CR list is being included in the contract. This will definitely save the project cost overrun at a later date if assumptions turn out to be false. So, don't forget to include the assumptions in the contract when the requirements list is also included in the contract.

Lesson 9.5

Do not forget to include assumptions in the contract that include the requirements list.

Compatibility plays a big role when designing software. In one of the projects, at the Presales stage, the customer wanted to use

WebSphere, a third-party software for our application. Their application was designed, or rather factory-tested, to work with a particular version.

Once moved to the contract signing stage, they decided to use WebLogic software. So, they asked the Sales person to replace WebSphere with WebLogic. At the macro level, both are middleware. So, from a sales perspective, it would not matter much. But from an application installation perspective; we were not prepared to make our program work with WebLogic. There was a huge hue and cry from the customer side. They claimed the software was supposed to be made compatible with WebLogic. While this change looked simple, end-to-end integration testing was required to ensure that it works well. Also, volume testing was already done on WebSphere and now doing it on WebLogic meant starting from scratch. Both software had a few different configuration properties. So, when we came to the execution stage, we discovered a huge gap. Not to mention the loss we made for this small mistake was not easily recoverable. But, considering that it was a Tier-1 customer, we agreed to take a hit. We made certain to make the software - WebLogic compatible with the required software. One needs to ensure that correct software and their versions are added in the contract and offshore validations and verification happen as per that. The final contract should be reviewed by the delivery team.

Lesson 9.6

Always review the list of exact software and their versions before signing the contract to avoid nasty surprises and late discovery. Add clause for change request if any deviations regarding software versions.

At the start of my career, I mostly worked on transformation projects in retail banking domain. We had to migrate data from the legacy system to our new core banking system. I had not yet had the chance to look at the contract, so I didn't know how the salesperson had included the migration-related details in the contract.

One of our customers was very adamant and rigid and used to object to every small issue and deviation. We had to prepare the migration scripts while the customer. The customer would extract the migration data from their legacy system. We didn't want to get entangled in the data extraction process from legacy system since only the customer's IT department knew the ins and outs of the legacy system.

We were in for a rude awakening.

When the data migration-related discussions started, the customer started talking about giving access to their systems and data structures. We were puzzled! Then the customer mentioned that data extraction was part of our responsibility along with data migration. At first, we denied it. When the customer insisted, we took a closer look at the contract.

The customer had added one sentence to the contract, which said that the vendor had to carry out data extraction besides data migration. While the salesperson was unaware of the implications of this seemingly small change, this single sentence *totally* changed the roles and responsibilities of the vendor. Besides, the delivery project manager was only in charge until the contract closure - this didn't protect our interests either.

We had a long discussion over the next few days to convince the customer. The customer remained adamant. They did not have the bandwidth and skillset to extract the data; moreover, this clause had been a deciding factor in awarding the contract to us.

After all, we were bound by the contract. We had to hire a couple of expensive resources with the relevant skills for data extraction. This hit our project's profitability by around six bps and was also a lesson learned the hard way. A single term can set you back by weeks, cutting down on revenue. Always ensure clarity when detailing roles and responsibilities on data migration in the contract.

Lesson 9.7

Ensure that data migration-related roles and responsibilities are clearly documented in the contract and taken care of in efforts estimation and commercials.

In one of my early projects, we had agreed to have a parallel run after the data migration. However, nobody mentioned the duration of the parallel run in the contract. It was just stated that the parallel run would be done until cutover.

The customer was not very tech-savvy. While the PM understood what a parallel run meant, he had underestimated its implications. It required tremendous preparation. Moreover, it required double the work as data had to be posted in the new as well as the legacy system. We had two choices: either hire new data entry operators trained to post the data in both systems or use the same user set to post in two different systems.

On top of this, we needed a way to validate if the posted data and the outputs were the same in both systems.

If we did this manually, the users might initially start out with enthusiasm, which might soon give way to tiredness and mistakes after a while. Without automation or additional hands, navigating such situations is difficult. It requires a *smart* solution.

Without a reconciliation mechanism in place, a wrong output could create a perception that the new system did not work as expected. This could result in a cascading or snowball effect over time that could make it difficult to figure out the root cause of an issue. Large gaps in financial or data mismatch could finally cause all hell to break loose.

If the project collapses and the customer's expectations aren't met, the onus to prove that the system works falls on the vendor PM. Unless the PM is smart, this may abruptly stop the parallel run. It can go into post-mortem mode while he figures out what is wrong. This results in losses for the client unless it is a T&M project.

Hence, one should always be clear about the duration of the parallel run and the strategy for data entry and verification. Unless this is not agreed upon without a plan, this is again another recipe for disaster.

Lesson 9.8

Record the contract's parallel run strategy, duration, mechanism, verification, and reconciliation in the contract. The parallel runs should be short since every deviation in the result has to be verified, after which corrective actions need to be taken, and the updated model has to be loaded for the next day.

Another one of my implementation projects involved data migration. Per the contract, the customer had to extract the data into a flat file and upload it into the new migrating system. The customer was confident about extracting the data quickly, and he did do it. Once the data files were uploaded, we didn't find many anomalies during the multiple mock runs in the test environment. The testing went well, and everything was going smoothly.

The final mock migration was planned a month before going live. This time, we would use the production data. We received the data and migrated it to the test environment. To our utter shock, we found several inconsistencies in the migrated data. This was a huge problem since we had never observed this during the test runs.

On further inquiry and analysis, we found a huge gap in terms of how data extraction was done. During the earlier testing, the extracted data was from the test environment, not the production environment. The client's migration team had hardcoded some core values into the data to fix the inconsistencies in the test environment's data. While our mock runs had gone smoothly, the real production data had too many serious discrepancies. This had happened despite specifications being shared with the customer upfront, explained in detail, and even signed off by the customer.

It took ten long weeks to rework the scripts before we were in a position to carry out mock runs. Christmas holidays delayed the plans by a month. Since critical resources were on planned leave, this derailed the budget, commercials, and the plan to go live.

Hence, one must be cautious while doing a mock migration run. Always ask the stakeholders how the data was extracted and even try to validate with source system although it's not your responsibility. Data migration is equivalent to 'garbage in, garbage out' unless data cleansing is not done.

Lesson 9.9

Ensure data cleansing is done and account for it in mock runs. Otherwise, it may cause serious troubles on the production cutover date.

If the application to be accessed by the bank's customers is outside their internal network (through a portal), security and penetration testing is required as a part of the compliance requirements. However, this is usually mentioned in just a few words in the contract. PMs can sometimes forget to plan support for security and penetration testing. This can cause a severe headache when it is time to go live.

In one of my implementations, we entered the last stage of UAT (UAT regression phase) when we realized that the customer had not completed the security testing. The production cutover date was just two weeks away. Some issues were raised with high and medium severity when security testing was performed. During discussions, the security testing consultant never highlighted that those issues needed to be fixed before we went live.

After the UAT was signed-off, the consultant suddenly mentioned that we could not go live without fixing those issues. We just had one weekend left. It was challenging to fix, test, and make a release. We weren't even sure if our proposed approach would be feasible for specific issues considering the integration with the bank's system. It took several long discussions to agree on deprioritizing it since the solution wasn't really clear. The team stretched over the weekend since the remaining stuff could be fixed.

From the PM's perspective, this was a total miss. It was not addressed or escalated on time. This is a common mistake: PMs can forget NFR issues like security or penetration testing that come on the critical path in the thick of testing.

Lesson 9.10

The PM should not lose sight of NFR testing. Those should be tracked with equal vigor before they come on a critical path.

Chapter Summary - SOW

The project contract defines the boundary of the project and drives the buyer and seller to perform and deliver services. An inappropriate contracting model may result in huge losses for both sides. Hence, it should be carefully selected after understanding the needs of the business holistically. It is always advisable to take a buy-in from all stakeholders and finalize the roles and responsibilities before signing the contract.

Similarly, the closure of the contract is equally important as a part of the project closure requirement. This requires someone to sign-off that all agreed deliverables have been delivered as per the specifications.

NOTES

CHAPTER 10

Lessons Learned

According to PMBOK, there has to be a lesson learnt repository for PM. However, hardly any project managers ask the management, QA, or their predecessors to share their experiences. The PM overlooks this in a hurry to prepare the plan, get resources on board, and start the project.

As they say, you should learn from others' mistakes. You can't live long enough to make them all yourself. Reading the contract or conducting a meeting with individual stakeholders is not enough - one should be able to go through the lessons from previous projects.

These are available in the company or group's repository, provided that management captures them before formally closing a project.

During handover, the new PM should meet the outgoing PM for advice on the project and ask for their experience managing similar projects. Predecessors might be reluctant to share lessons due to fear of being perceived as inefficient. However, the new PM should always keep the success of the current project in mind. One way to do this is to ask the outgoing PM what they would do differently if the project had to start all over. Seasoned predecessors are usually more cooperative when talking about their experiences.

A few lessons I learned are:

- Ensure a balanced team in terms of experienced resources. Never try to execute a project with all freshers or an all-new team. It is very difficult to stick to this core principle that is prevalent in all organizations. But one has to convince management about the implications of the project failure due to less experienced resources. There shouldn't be more than 20-30% freshers on the team. Otherwise, you are at the risk of making them learn as well as deliver. This will ultimately prove disastrous as the project progresses. Minor delays may snowball into missing timelines or poor quality, which may eventually hit back at the PM and the sponsor. Highlight this in a weekly status report or flag it as high risk.
- Continuous regression testing at offshore arrests the issues early. The code drop or release may be rushed to avoid penalties and meet the committed deadlines. It is possible that the first code drop may not be very well tested. Hence, it is advisable to continue offshore testing to ensure you are one step ahead of the customer.
- Past issues faced with the customer's different teams help accurately estimate phase-wise timelines in the project plan. Some customers have weak infrastructure teams. Some customers do not invest in good administrators like DBA, MQ admin, etc.
- Bottlenecks during project execution can force you to resolve issues even if they do not belong to your application. Proving that the application does not cause the issue can take significant time and energy.
- Expectations on perfection may vary based on customers and geography, to customer. From my experience in Japan, 99% perfection is still considered as bad as 90% or lesser -

they expect 100% perfection on the first attempt. Customers in other regions have better tolerance levels at 80-90% perfection, which is much appreciated. Hence, always take a cue from past lessons while dealing with a customer to plan the deliverables.

Lesson 10.1

All lessons learned from past executions can be considered while project planning and resource budgeting, which save time and money to ensure the successful and timely completion of the project.

Chapter Summary - Lessons learnt

This is one of the most ignored parts of the project execution. Even before the project reaches the closure phase, the team already has their next assignment. At times, they even do not get time to take a break or rejuvenate. In a hurry to start the next project, the PM finds it too overwhelming to document the lessons learnt if the project has been successfully executed. It should be the sponsor's responsibility to get the learnings from the PM documented before he moves on to the next project, LOB or organization. The lessons learned should the document good, bad and ugly lessons since the beginning of the project execution. It should clearly document what could have been done differently if the same project was required to be executed again. Also, it should contribute any new or customized templates, processes or information that contributed to the success of the project. This should be done in a formal setting with key stakeholders for everyone to understand nuances of the lessons learned.

In addition, when a project starts, PM should first of all refer to the lessons learned for the similar project in the past.

NOTES

Praise for the book

There are many books in the market on Project Management, its theories and practices. Some are text books and some are case studies. So, you may say this is one more. Yes, this is one more but in a totally different direction.

This book provides a categorized enlisting of author's experience on his more than 25 years of experience as a project manager and in project management. Primarily, his domain knowledge of core banking is crucial. He has enlisted various conditions under which he faced: the customer on one side, his own team members on the other side, and complex modern and traditional organizations on both sides.

As he has mentioned in the introduction of the book, this is for novices and also for seasoned project management professionals who are facing issues at every stage, helping them resolve situations amicably in favour of the customer with a win-win at the end.

This book is a path breaking trend on project management for working project management professionals. I am sure every reader of these pages would find that his heart beats in it at one or more places.

Wish you a happy reading.

- Bharat Bhagat

Past PMI Mumbai chapter President

Project analysis is a highly required and recommended program for any project-driven company. It has been rightly observed and recorded by the author that quite a few projects fail due to the wrong estimation, information collection, understanding of requirements of the customer, or improper documentation. These areas have been rightly pointed out by the author with some implementable suggestions.

This book can work as a wonderful guide for companies who work on improper estimations and finally end up bankrupt or deliver substandard quality, ruining further scope of earning business. There are too many organizations that work on instincts. They do not bother to spend time acquiring the right data from the customer and tend to work more on assumptions. The chapters in this book will serve as a guide to such management to prevent disasters in their respective organizations. This book can also serve as a guide for clients to provide the right information to their vendors if they want to have qualitative work delivered to them within stipulated timeframes and budgets. For proper implementation of projects and to achieve the right kind of value for money, both the client and the vendor should understand the requirements of each other clearly.

Proper documentation is also a necessity to ensure proper implementation. Every important matter should be clearly documented and recorded for the sake of clarity and smooth implementation. There are many methods to implement a particular project. The choice of the method of execution and the proper tool depends on the correct understanding of the needs of the customer and adequate estimation for the project. The clarity in estimation depends on the collection of proper data and derivatives. Therefore, project managers should first focus on deriving the optimum efforts in these areas from their team of marketing / estimation.

This book is highly recommended for all project companies and not only to companies in IT. The points covered in this book are the most desired points that are required to run a project company.

- SATADAL LAHIRI
(Exponent of TOC, Eliyahu Goldratt Foundation, Israel)

The author has done a really good job. It is a much-needed book on a very relevant topic which is very much helpful for those readers who want to know the practical aspect of Project Management.

It's written in a very simple and straightforward language that everyone can understand. There is not much complicated technical language used in this book so anyone can read and understand it very well and practice. I found very interesting pictures/stories and quotes in this book which logically put in and create a curiosity in it. The first picture itself made me read this book interestingly and continuously.

Author Mr. Parekh has put his insights in this book beautifully about project management and its practical aspects of it.

The famous quote says" "Knowledge is potential power, Knowledge without action is like a Bird without Wings". This is what exactly Author Mr. Parekh has applied in this book. The reader will get all tools or ideas from this book which can be activated or utilized as per your needs.

This well-researched content along with the author's life experiences is aptly put forward to make it relevant in each chapter. This book is for everyone who wants to learn and implement Project Management.

This book is filled with valuable insights and practical pieces of advice. Do yourself a favor. Read this book and lead your projects trouble-free and smoothly always!

- Dr. Ravindran K A

A Management Professional, Certified Life Coach & Author

This book written by Biren contains his rich and varied experiences in the IT field. He has standardized and globalized the knowledge and lessons learnt so that they are not only his experiences, but are generic for the IT world. Academics to corporate and again ploughing back the corporate experiences into the academics is a great initiative. Tacit knowledge is converted into operational knowledge for young professionals. Such literature makes the information technology knowledge base richer and richer. The usage is in academics and in corporate too.

- Dr Abhay Juvekar

Quality Manager

www.ingramcontent.com/pod-product-compliance
Lightning Source LLC
LaVergne TN
LVHW041110150826
845673LV00007B/2000

* 9 7 8 9 3 9 4 8 0 8 0 8 9 *